Argentina

Chile

Paraguay

Uruguay

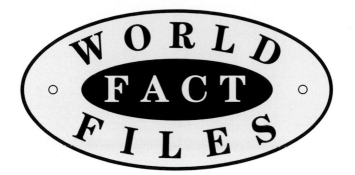

ARGENTINA ✻ CHILE
PARAGUAY ✻ URUGUAY

Anna Selby

MACDONALD YOUNG BOOKS

First published in 1999 by Macdonald Young Books
An imprint of Wayland Publishers Ltd
© Macdonald Young Books 1999

Macdonald Young Books
61 Western Road
Hove
East Sussex
BN3 1JD

Find Macdonald Young Books on the Internet at
http://www.myb.co.uk

Design and typesetting Roger Kohn Designs
Commissioning editor Rosie Nixon
Editor Merle Thompson
Picture research Shelley Noronha
Maps János Márffy

We are grateful to the following for permission
to reproduce photographs:
Front Cover: Robert Harding, *above* (L Murray);
Robert Harding, *below* (C Bowman);
Cephos, page 39 (R & K Muschenetz); Sylvia Corday, pages
10/11 (J Smith); Eye Ubiquitous, pages 8, 41 *above left*
(N Wisciman); Robert Harding, pages 19 (C Bowman), 28
(R Frerck), 30 (R Frerck), 42 (R McLeod); Hutchinson
Libraries, page 15 (M Friend); Impact, pages 24 (C Penn) 26
(H Hughes); Roger Kohn, page 38 *below right*; Panos, pages
25 *above right* (C Sattlberger), 32 (H Hughes), 44 (Julio
Etchart); Popperfoto, pages 27, 45 (G Cameron, Reuters);
Rex Features, pages 21 (P Heim Sath), 22 (F Arias), 31;
South American Pictures, pages 12 (K Jarvis),14
(T Morrison), 16 (T Morrison), 17 (T Morrison), 18 *below right*
(R Francis), 20 (T Morrison), 29 (R Francis), 33 (T Morrison),
36 *above left* and *below right* (T Morrison), 38 *above left*
(P Dixon), 40 (T Morrison), 41 *below right* (T Morrison), 43
above left (T Morrison); Still Pictures, page 18 *above left*
(Julio Etchart); Tony Stone, pages 13 (A Smith), 34/35
(R Van Der Hilst); Topham Picturepoint, pages 9, 25 *below*,
35; Trip, pages 23 (M Barlow), 43 *below right* (E Smith);
WPL, page 37.

The statistics given in this book are the most up to date
available at the time of going to press

Printed in Hong Kong by Wing King Tong

A CIP catalogue record for this book is available from
the British Library

ISBN: 0 7500 2619 7

CONTENTS

Words that are explained in the glossary are printed in
SMALL CAPITALS the first time they are mentioned in the text.

INTRODUCTION

The four countries that form the southern part of the South American continent are very different from each other. These are the Republic of Paraguay, rural and LAND-LOCKED; the tiny eastern Republic of Uruguay, the third smallest state in South America after French Guiana and Surinam; the vast, Europeanized Argentine Republic; and the long, narrow Republic of Chile, squeezed between the Andes mountains and the Pacific Ocean. In total, these countries cover 4,108,000 square kilometres, which is almost half the land area of the United States and around twelve times the size of the United Kingdom. Their total populations amount to over 55,000,000 people.

This is a land of great variety. The Andes mountains run the entire length of the continent of South America. Some of the peaks rise to over 6,500 metres, and many have glaciers and snowfields. There are, however, some areas in the more northern parts where tropical climates and even deserts can be found.

Farming is vital to the economies of all four countries and most of their exports are based on agricultural products. These vary widely from the cotton and timber of Paraguay to Argentina's huge exports of meat, sugar and grains. Chile is alone

▼ *The 67-metre high obelisk in the Plaza de la Republica is a familiar landmark in the centre of the busy Avenido 9 de Julio, in Argentina's capital, Buenos Aires.*

among the four in having important mineral resources. It is the world's leading producer of copper and a major supplier of precious metals.

In the past, however, the plentiful resources of these countries have not meant that their economies have been successful. This is because they have been undermined by unstable government. The people have suffered military dictatorships, COUPS, revolutions, civil wars and assassinations. Also, in 1982, Argentina went to war with the UK about the ownership of the Falkland Islands, or 'Las Malvinas', as they are called in Argentina. All of these problems have led to huge inflation and massive foreign debts. Within recent years, however, the whole area has become more stable. The economies of each country have improved, and governments, for the most part, have become more liberal and democratic.

● Population density: Argentina has 12 people per square kilometre; Chile has 18; Uruguay, 17; and Paraguay 11

● Capital cities: Buenos Aires, Argentina, 10,728,000; Santiago, Chile, 4,858,000; Asunción, Paraguay, 729,000; Montevideo, Uruguay, 1,248,000

● Highest peak: Aconcagua in Argentina, 6,960 metres. It is the highest mountain outside Asia

● Major languages: Spanish is the main language of all four countries. However, 40% of Paraguayans speak Guaraní and, in Argentina, there is also some Guaraní spoken as well as a little Italian and Welsh

● Major religions: Argentina, 93% Roman Catholic and 2% Protestant; Chile, 80% Roman Catholic and 6% Protestant; Paraguay, 96% Roman Catholic; Uruguay, 60% Roman Catholic, 3% Protestant and 2% Jewish

● Major resources: copper ore, iron ore, limestone, precious metal ores, oil, hydro-electricity, timber, fish

● Major products: meat, wool, wine, cotton, oil seeds

● Environmental problems: DEFORESTATION, water pollution

◀ *A typical Paraguayan farmhouse at Caaguazú, in rural eastern Paraguay.*

9

THE LANDSCAPE

South America's landscape is one of extremes. For instance, Argentina is the eighth largest country in the world, and is only slightly smaller than the entire Indian sub-continent. The enormous range of altitudes and latitudes means that there are endless variations in the region's landscape – from high plains to subtropical lowlands, from the flat PAMPAS to volcanic peaks and mountains, from tropical forest to glaciers and from deserts to frozen fjords. Chile and Argentina are divided by the huge mountain chain of the Andes, which runs from the north of Argentina to the south, before finally disappearing into the cold depths of the South Atlantic Ocean. The soaring volcanic peaks of the Andes tower over the high, arid Andean steppe, or ALTIPLANO, dotted with saline lakes, called salares, all over 4,000 metres high. East of the Andes, in northern Argentina, the lowlands alternate between open SAVANNAS and swampy lowland forests. Further south, the pampas takes

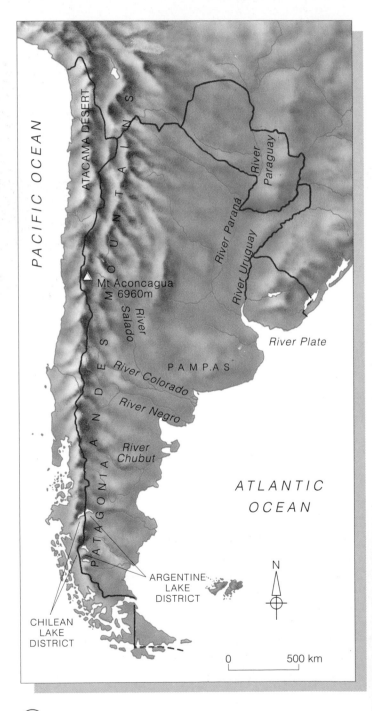

over. This is an endless flat plain, now mostly farmland or cattle ranches. Below the pampas, is the huge region of Patagonia, which has the same name both sides of the Andes, whether in Chile or Argentina. There are glaciers on the eastern, Argentinan side, but the most dramatic landscape is to be found on the Chilean side of the mountains. Here, there are snow-capped volcanoes, impenetrably thick forests and rocky, windswept, uninhabited islands. These form part of the Chilean fjords that extend all the way south to Cape Horn.

Central Chile consists of a series of fertile river basins known collectively as the Central Valley. Most of the population live in

KEY FACTS

● Chile is more than ten times as long as it is wide.
● Pampa is a South American Indian word meaning a flat, featureless expanse of land.
● Tierra del Fuego, at the southernmost tip of South America, has a cold, bleak climate, but its name means 'land of fire'. It got its name because the fires lit by the original inhabitants of the island were spotted by the early European sailors on their voyages of discovery.
● Paraguay is bordered mostly by rivers, including the Paraná in the south and east (South America's second longest river) and the Paraguay in the north-west.
● From its northernmost to its southernmost points, Argentina stretches as far as the distance from Scotland to the Sahara Desert.

this area. Further north is the Atacama Desert, one of the driest places on Earth.

Chile also has various groups of islands, or archipelagos, in the Pacific, including the famous Easter Island (Rapa Nui) which is 3,790 kilometres from the coast. This is known throughout the world for its unique moai, or huge stone figures. All of these islands were produced by the action of underwater volcanoes. Easter Island's triangular shape was formed, for example, by the meeting of three separate lava flows. Volcanic activity and frequent

◀ *The pampas in Argentinian Patagonia. Most of the best pampas land has been enclosed for horse and cattle ranches or for crop cultivation.*

earthquakes are still commonplace, especially in the south of Chile. On occasion, coastal towns have been wiped out by tidal waves.

Although it is one of South America's smallest countries, Uruguay is still large when compared to European countries. It is around the size of England and Wales or the state of North Dakota in the USA. It shares borders with both Brazil and

Argentina and has a scenic Atlantic Ocean coastline. Less fertile than the Argentine pampas, its rolling hills are very similar to those of southern Brazil on its north-eastern border. It is famed in South America for its beautiful beaches, as well as dunes, headlands and vast lagoons.

Paraguay is the northernmost of the four countries, and borders Brazil, Bolivia and Argentina. It has no coast, and the capital,

◀ *The Torres del Paine National Park, in Chilean Patagonia, has some of the most spectacular scenery in the world. Torres is the Spanish word for 'towers' and describes the shape of these ice-capped mountains.*

▼ *The Iguazú Falls on the border of Argentina and Brazil are more than 2 kilometres wide. Over 5,000 cubic metres of water plunge down the 70-metre drop every second.*

Asunción, is connected to the Atlantic only by the Rivers Paraguay and Paraná. It is about the same size as Germany or the American state of California. Half of the country is covered in forest and much of it is sub-tropical. Compared to other South American countries, it is quite low lying, rising only to 600 metres. In the west of the country is the Gran Chaco, a vast plain that stretches to the Bolivian border. This now consists mostly of huge ranches or ESTANCIAS. This area is almost deserted with only 4% of the population living there.

CLIMATE AND WEATHER

As Argentina, Chile, Paraguay and Uruguay are all in the southern hemisphere, their summers occur during the months of November to March and their winters from May to September. However, because of the vast range of altitudes and latitudes within the area, the four countries all have very different climates. There are also very great variations within each individual country.

In Chile, for instance, the Atacama Desert in the north has soaring daytime temperatures that, in the summer, average 35°C. It is so dry that no plant or animal life can exist. In the same area, however, the early mornings can be extremely cold before the fierce sun causes the temperatures to rise again. In total contrast, the south of the country has

virtually continuous cold weather, with some of the stormiest conditions in the world. In Tierra del Fuego, the island at the southern tip of the continent that belongs partly to Chile and partly to Argentina, the winter average temperature is 4°C. Even in the summer, it rises only to 11°C. Around the capital of Santiago, however, there is mostly a pleasant Mediterranean climate.

Chile also has extremely high altitudes and, in the mountains, there is snow for most of the year. In the winter, the passes leading to Argentina and Bolivia are frequently blocked. In fact, in the Chilean Andes there is enough snow for skiing for five months of the year — often while the coast is basking in the sun not much more than 150 kilometres away. Because the

▼ *Cantegril Beach, Punta del Este, Uruguay, one of the country's popular sandy beaches.*

▶ *Many people go skiing in the winter to popular resorts in the Andes, like Bariloche, in Argentina.*

mountains are so high, the ultra-violet rays of the sun can cause severe sunburn and many people suffer from soroche, or altitude sickness.

Uruguay, by contrast, has one of the most agreeable and mild climates in the southern hemisphere. It is warm, even in the winter, and frosts are very rare. The summers are quite dry by South American standards, and reliably hot without the temperatures soaring to uncomfortable levels. Together with its beaches, this climate has made Uruguay a favourite holiday destination for South Americans from all over the continent.

KEY FACTS

● There are areas in northern Chile's Atacama Desert where no rainfall has ever been recorded.
● During the summer in Paraguay, it is very hot and humid. This is the time when most rain falls, and in the capital Asunción there can be as much as 20 mm of rainfall a day.
● South of Buenos Aires, there are few ports in Argentina because the tidal range along the Atlantic coast is so great that it is unsafe for shipping.

Western Paraguay, on the other hand, has a hot, humid climate all year round, with summer temperatures averaging an uncomfortable 35°C. In the winter, the temperatures are mild, but sudden cold fronts, known as pamperos, sweep up from Argentina in the spring and autumn, causing temperatures to drop very suddenly — up to 20°C in just a few hours. The eastern part of the country has even higher summer temperatures of around 40°C, and the scant rain evaporates quickly in the heat. The area's agriculture, therefore, has to depend on irrigation rather than rainfall.

Chile is a much wetter country than Argentina as rain, sweeping in from the Pacific Ocean to the west, falls here first as

▲ *Although it has a very inhospitable climate, the Atacama Desert has been populated for long periods. Thousands of years ago, Andean Indians settled here along the coast, to fish for their food.*

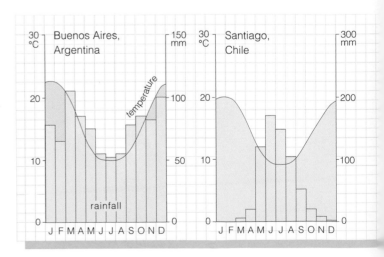

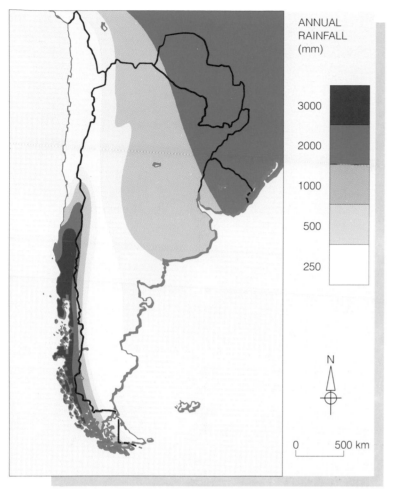

ANNUAL
RAINFALL
(mm)

3000

2000

1000

500

250

N

0   500 km

▶ *The Iguazú River flows through the lush rainforest in the north of Argentina, close to the border with Brazil.*

the rain-clouds are forced to rise over the Andes. In the altiplano, or high plain, in the far north of Argentina, it is arid and irrigation is needed for farming. However, in the summer, there can be sudden rainstorms with flash flooding and even snow. Rainfall increases steadily further south and on the pampas, south of Buenos Aires, the small rivers often flood. This problem is made worse by the almost uniformly flat terrain. Argentinian Patagonia is much drier than the Chilean side of the Andes but, in the extreme south, this does not prevent there being sufficient snow to produce the largest glaciers in the southern hemisphere outside Antarctica.

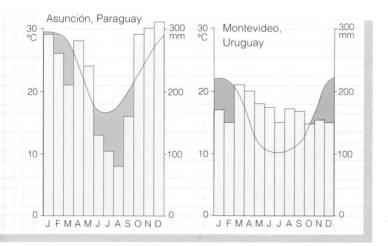

Asunción, Paraguay

30
°C

20

10

0
J F M A M J J A S O N D

300
mm

200

100

0

Montevideo,
Uruguay

30
°C

20

10

0
J F M A M J J A S O N D

300
mm

200

100

0

NATURAL RESOURCES

The mighty Itaipú Dam, a joint Brazilian–Paraguayan project, which has enabled Paraguay to produce 99.8% of the electricity it needs.

to Chile, it has also made its economy dependent on the world prices for minerals. So, when these dipped in the 1981 world recession, Chile went through a period of severe economic decline. The economy is now, however, generally much recovered.

Chile also has abundant reserves of oil, natural gas and coal and Argentina, too, is self-sufficient in petroleum and other energy resources. However, Argentina, which is one of the wealthiest countries in Latin America, has failed to make the most of these.

This is because the country has suffered from political upheavals and serious

Most of Chile's oil comes from the extreme south of the country. This oil drilling platform is at Punta Arenas, in the Straits of Magellan.

Although the name 'Argentina' means 'land of silver', it is only Chile out of these four countries that has great mineral wealth. It produces huge amounts of copper and also has vast reserves of iron ore, manganese, lead, gold, silver, zinc, molybdenum, sulphur and nitrates. It is the leading exporter of precious metal ores. In 1996, the world's total exports were valued at US$ 337,600,000. Chile exported US$ 61,700,000 worth of precious ores, compared to US$ 8,200,000 worth by the United States and US$ 35,000,000 worth by the entire European Union. However, while this natural wealth is very important

◀ *The Chuquicamata copper mine is in the north of Chile in the Atacama Desert, and is built on a vast scale. It employs 9,000 people and the ore is extracted from a pit 4 kilometres long, 2 kilometres wide and 630 metres deep. Every day, 60,000 tons of ore are processed.*

mismanagement of the economy.

Uruguay and Paraguay are both extremely poor in terms of mineral resources. Paraguay, however, has now begun to use its rivers to produce hydro-

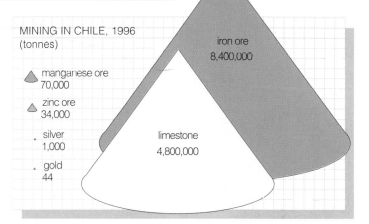

MINING IN CHILE, 1996 (tonnes)

▲ manganese ore 70,000

▲ zinc ore 34,000

. silver 1,000

. gold 44

iron ore 8,400,000

limestone 4,800,000

KEY FACTS

● Today, Chuquicamata is a huge, modern copper mine, but copper has been mined here from very early times, even before the INCAS arrived.

● Although the Itaipú Dam has given Paraguay great benefits in energy resources, it has caused an environmental disaster. By creating a reservoir of 1,350 square kilometres, 200 metres deep, it has produced an area of stagnant water that has given anopheles mosquitos a new breeding ground. This has brought malaria back to an area from which it had virtually disappeared.

● In 1995, Chile produced 2.56 million tonnes of copper ore, over a quarter of the world's total production of 10.01 million tonnes.

electric power. As it is such a poor country, it has needed the help of its neighbours to do this. The Itaipú Dam, which harnessed the potential of the mighty River Paraná, is the world's largest hydro-electric project, with a capacity of 12.6 million kilowatts. The whole venture cost US$25 billion and was built with Brazilian finance. The result is that Paraguay now generates almost all of its electricity from water power, and has some left over to export to Brazil. However, the project has left Paraguay with an increased foreign debt, because of maintenance costs and repayments for its share of the capital.

South America is a very sparsely populated region compared to much of the rest of the world. This is partly because some areas are uninhabitable due to their climate or geographical position. However, it is also because the waves of immigration over the centuries have never been continuous. The population, once settled, has generally grown very slowly.

The descendants of the original native people, in most cases, make up only a very small proportion of the population. When the first CONQUISTADORES arrived in the 16th century, the native peoples had been isolated from the diseases of the rest of the world for at least 10,000 years. Consequently, in much of the region, the arrival of Europeans reduced the local population by up to 95%. This was due, not so much to mistreatment, but to contact with smallpox, influenza, typhus and other diseases to which they had no resistance.

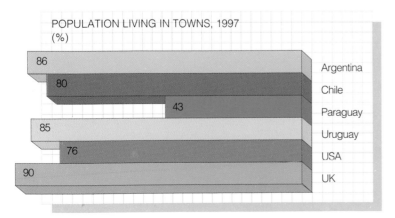

POPULATION LIVING IN TOWNS, 1997
(%)

86	Argentina
80	Chile
43	Paraguay
85	Uruguay
76	USA
90	UK

◀ *Calle Florida, part of Buenos Aires'*
busy shopping area, reflects the city's
European feel, and features many of
Europe's most sophisticated shops.

POPULATION DENSITY, 1997
(per sq km)

13	Argentina
19	Chile
12	Paraguay
18	Uruguay
331	Japan
283	India
238	UK

There are now small groups of
pure descendants from the original
inhabitants living all over the region.
However, the size of their communities is
insignificant, when compared to the
numbers of European or mestizo people –
those of mixed European and Indian
ancestry. In Argentina, the country's
INDIGENOUS POPULATION numbers 100,000,
but this includes several different groups,
including the Quechua and the Mapuche.
Argentina had a policy of promoting

European immigration in the 19th century
and modelling itself on Europe. The new
settlers quickly displaced the Indians.
Not all of them were of Spanish origin and
many came from Italy, Wales, England,
Germany, the Ukraine and the Basque

▶ *President*
Carlos Menem of
Argentina is of
Syrian descent.
He is the most
prominent of a
small group of
immigrants from
the Middle East
to have gained
political influence.
Although now a
Roman Catholic –
a necessary
requirement for
presidency – he
was originally a
Moslem.

POPULATION

region. Some of these immigrants to Argentina have preserved something of their culture. This is particularly true of the Welsh in Chubut province where, until recently, Welsh was the second language, and appeared on signposts alongside the Spanish. Buenos Aires also has a large Jewish community, and there has been an influx of immigrants from the Middle East, including the country's President, Carlos Menem. Most people in Argentina live in cities – a third of them in Buenos Aires. This is also true of Chile and Uruguay, although Paraguay has a much more rural population.

In Paraguay, less than half the population live in towns and the capital, Asunción, has only 729,000 people living

▼ *A Chilean band with traditional instruments, playing in the street to celebrate a FIESTA marking an eclipse of the sun.*

KEY FACTS

● There have been so many Italian immigrants to Argentina that there are now more Italian surnames in the Buenos Aires area than Spanish ones.
● Buenos Aires has the eighth largest Jewish community in the world (400,000) but it has been the focus of terrorist bombing. There were explosions in the Israeli Embassy in 1992 and a Jewish cultural centre in 1994, when many people were killed.
● Uruguay is South America's smallest Spanish-speaking country.
● The Mapuche of Chile were famed as silversmiths long before the arrival of the Spanish Conquistadors and they continue to make their exquisite artefacts today.
● For a long time, the inhabitants of Easter Island in the Pacific Ocean were thought to be of South American origin. It is now accepted that they are Polynesian and that they are related to the Maori of New Zealand and the islanders of the Pacific, such as the Tahitians and Tongans.

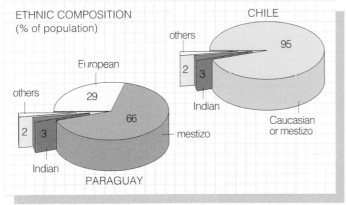

ETHNIC COMPOSITION
(% of population)

European

others

29

2 3

66 mestizo

Indian

PARAGUAY

CHILE

others

95

2 3

Indian

Caucasian
or mestizo

▲ *Guaraní Indians in Asunción, the capital of Paraguay, selling local handicrafts.*

pure Europeans, speaks Guaraní as well as Spanish. There is a small population (about 3%) of pure Indians, mostly living in the Chaco region. Some, until very recently, followed their traditional way of life of hunting and gathering.

Although Uruguay's agriculture is vital to its economy, the vast majority of the population live in cities, nearly half of them in the capital, Montevideo. The original people, the Charruas, have almost died out, although there is a tiny mestizo population close to the Brazilian border. Most Uruguayans are of European extraction,

there. Unlike Argentina, where the Indian population declined and the Europeans took over, in Paraguay the original inhabitants, the Guaraní, absorbed the Spanish settlers. As a result, the population is now 66% mestizo, and the entire population, including upper-class

mainly Italian and Spanish. There is also a small population of people of mixed African and Uruguayan blood. These are descended from slaves brought to the country in the 19th century.

There are only a few people of full-blooded European ancestry in Chile. The great majority of Chileans are mestizo — of mixed Spanish and Indian extraction. Within this mix, people regard themselves as being 'mostly European' or 'mostly Indian' but there is less racial diversity here than in most South American countries. A small population of Africans led to the formation of another racial group, the mulattos. They have mixed black and European ancestors, while

▲ *In the mid-19th century, there was a large influx of Welsh farmers who settled in Patagonia. They have retained their cultural identity for more than a hundred years, as can be seen in this very Welsh tea party.*

zambos are of black and Indian blood. Unlike Argentina, which absorbed many groups of immigrants from Europe during the 19th century, Chile had very few. Those who did come included Germans, French, Italians and Yugoslavs. There is still a small Indian population including the Mapuche, the Aymara and the Rapa Nui of Easter Island.

DAILY LIFE

The long history of political and financial upheavals has left many South Americans feeling uncertain about many of the basics of day-to-day life that people of other countries just take for granted. Argentina, for example, suffered from runaway inflation that, at its worst, was over 3,000%. At this rate, the price of a loaf of bread increased by 8% every day. Moreover, during the worst days of political repression, many political prisoners were taken who were never heard of again. Now, however, all four countries appear to be more stable, both in terms of political freedom and in their economies. Because of this, people are able to conduct their lives with greater certainty about the future than they have for decades.

▼ *The vast sheep and cattle estancias of Argentina are run by gauchos, the cowboys of South America.*

PEOPLE WITHOUT ACCESS TO SAFE WATER, 1990–96 (% of population)

Argentina	Paraguay	Uruguay
29	58	25

▼ *Gauchos barbecuing meat on an open fire as they journey with their animals to fresh pastures.*

HEALTH

Standards of healthcare vary throughout South America. Argentina has a good public healthcare system while, in Uruguay, cash payment is often necessary before the sick are allowed into hospital. There are a number of diseases that are still quite common in South America that have been wiped out in more developed countries. These include typhoid, polio, cholera and, in some areas, malaria.

One of the main health problems is a lack of clean drinking water. In major cities, the water is often – but not always – safe to drink but, in the countryside, it is often contaminated. Also, food may not be

▲ *A polo match in Buenos Aires. Polo is the national game of Argentina.*

▶ *The footballer, Diego Maradona, becomes a national hero when Argentina wins the World Cup in Mexico City, in 1986.*

prepared hygienically either in the towns or countryside, so dysentery is also widespread.

RELIGION

All four countries are predominantly Roman Catholic, the religion brought by the Conquistadores. However, the official religion is often tinged with local superstitions, depending on the region. In rural Paraguay, for instance, many people are said to regard their local parish priest as a healer or even a magician. There are many religious festivals in South America, often celebrated with processions, music and feasting. People often dress in special costumes and carry religious statues through the streets.

In Chile, Evangelical Protestantism has grown rapidly, the largest new church being the Pentecostal Methodist Church. Evangelical Protestantism has also made great inroads in Argentina, where television evangelists are popular. Roman Catholicism is still the state religion,

KEY FACTS

● In Paraguay, children between the ages of 10 and 14 make up almost 8% of the workforce.
● South America not only produces a great deal of the world's wine, they drink a lot of it, too. Argentina, Chile and Uruguay are all in the world's top twenty countries of wine drinkers – France comes first in the table.
● Argentinians have many television stations to choose from. There are 32 private stations, 10 state ones and 2 run by universities – 44 in all.
● Chile produces beautiful jewellery, using silver and lapis lazuli, a bright blue stone which is found only here and in Afghanistan.

DAILY LIFE

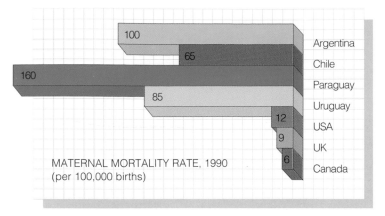

100	Argentina
65	Chile
160	Paraguay
85	Uruguay
12	USA
9	UK
6	Canada

MATERNAL MORTALITY RATE, 1990
(per 100,000 births)

nonetheless, and President Menem had to convert from Islam before he was able to become leader. However, the Roman Catholic Church received a great deal of criticism in the 1970s and 1980s when it was seen to be supporting the military government, infamous for its torture and murder.

EDUCATION

In Argentina, education is free and compulsory from ages 5–12. There is also a good public secondary school system that follows the French model, in which all subjects are compulsory. Tertiary education in universities and teacher training colleges is also free. Argentina's literacy rate of 94% is one of the highest in South America.

In Chile, 90% of the adult population can read and write. Elementary education is free for at least eight years. There is both public and private secondary education, although many children leave school early to work and help support the family. In Uruguay, primary education is also free and compulsory. Enrolment in the free secondary schools is also high, although this is not compulsory. In Paraguay, school is compulsory only until age 12, and the

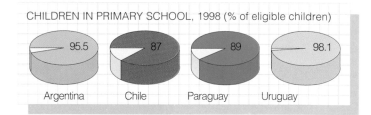

CHILDREN IN PRIMARY SCHOOL, 1998 (% of eligible children)

95.5	87	89	98.1
Argentina	Chile	Paraguay	Uruguay

◀ **Tango is the national dance of Argentina. In the 1930s, when it first became popular, people would often dance it in the streets. This demonstration is taking place at San Telmo, the Sunday Antiques market in Buenos Aires.**

◄ *South Americans often celebrate religious and secular holidays with processions and pageants. This is the Fiesta de Cuasimodo procession in Chile's capital, Santiago.*

country has one of the lowest literacy rates in South America of 81%.

LEISURE

In many ways, Argentina has a very Europeanized culture. The spectacular Teatro Colón in Buenos Aires (named after Christopher Columbus, whose name in Spanish is Colón) opened in 1908 as one of the foremost opera houses in the world. In musical terms, however, Argentina is probably best known for its national dance, the tango, still the most commonly heard music in the country. In Chile, the most famous dance is the Cueca – in which handkerchiefs are waved to the accompaniment of guitar, harp and handclapping.

South America is also famous for its writers, notably Jorge Luis Borges and Manuel Puig of Argentina, the Chilean poet Pablo Neruda, the Paraguayan poet and novelist Augusto Roa Bastos and Juan Carlos Onetti, the Uruguayan novelist.

FESTIVALS AND HOLIDAYS IN CHILE	
1 January	NEW YEAR'S DAY
March/April	EASTER
1 May	LABOUR DAY
21 May	NAVY DAY
15 August	THE ASSUMPTION
18-19 September	INDEPENDENCE DAYS
12 October	DISCOVERY OF AMERICA
1 November	ALL SAINTS' DAY
8 December	THE IMMACULATE CONCEPTION
25 December	CHRISTMAS DAY

Theatre is popular in all four countries and Argentina has a flourishing film industry.

Sport is very popular throughout the region, particularly football, at which South Americans excel. Argentina is famous for its world-class polo teams and its polo ponies. The ponies are renowned for their speed and ability to change direction at the slightest touch from their riders. It has also produced many world-class sports personalities, such as the tennis player, Gabriela Sabatini and Juan Manuel Fangio, considered by many to be the greatest racing driver of all time. He won the World Grand Prix Championship five times in the 1950s.

RULE AND LAW

At some time in the last few decades, all South American countries have experienced political repression and upheavals on a grand scale. Military dictatorships, coups, revolutions and civil wars have all meant very real danger in the lives of ordinary people. Books could be censored and removed, and there was no freedom of expression. Even large family gatherings, such as birthday parties, could be regarded with suspicion and require police approval before they could take place. People who ignored any of these rules would be imprisoned and often 'disappear'. In Argentina, during the JUNTA or military dictatorship of the 1970s and early 1980s, there were officially 9,000 cases of such disappearances. In these instances, people were tortured, illegally imprisoned and eventually murdered – although unofficial estimates are three times this number.

Even before this, however, Argentina had been at the mercy of corrupt, unjust or ineffectual government for many years. The country's most famous rulers were undoubtedly the Peróns. Juan Carlos was the President, but his wife, Eva, best

▼ ***Los Madres de los Desaparecidos – or the mothers of the disappeared – in Buenos Aires, where they march in front of the presidential palace in memory of their children murdered in the 1970s and early 1980s.***

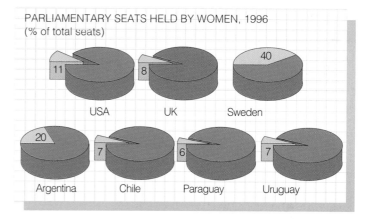

◀ *Eva Perón first came to politics as the wife of President Juan Perón but her charismatic public speaking soon gave her a special role in Argentine politics. Her death in 1952 traumatized the entire country.*

PARLIAMENTARY SEATS HELD BY WOMEN, 1996
(% of total seats)

11	8	40
USA	UK	Sweden

20	7	6	7
Argentina	Chile	Paraguay	Uruguay

known as 'Evita', had just as much popular support. While Perón was elected by democratic vote, he then went on to change the constitution. He abolished the clause prohibiting the re-election of a president and, in 1952, he was elected for a second six-year term. He was, however, unable to control galloping inflation and the country slipped further and further into debt to foreign nations. His regime collapsed in 1955. A series of short-lived presidents and military juntas followed until the military took over in 1966. They held power until 1973, when the country was torn by riots and Perón returned briefly as president. He died the following year and his regime, led by his widow, was overthrown by the military junta in 1976.

This junta was to collapse because of the 1982 war with Britain over the Falkland Islands, known in Argentina as 'Las Malvinas'. While this war had great national support initially, it collapsed after

KEY FACTS

● One of the most distinguished South American politicians was Uruguay's José Batlle y Ordóñez. In the first two decades of the 20th century, he organized the first welfare state in the continent, including pensions, unemployment benefits and limits on the length of the working day.

● Eva Perón was an actress before she married the president. Women were given the vote in 1947 because of her influence. Today, Argentina has one of the best records in the world for the number of women in politics, with a very high percentage of parliamentary seats held by women.

● Chile won its independence from Spain in the early 19th century under the command of an Irish-Chilean called Bernardo O'Higgins. He became the head of the first Chilean government. There is a street in Santiago named after him – Avenida Bernardo O'Higgins.

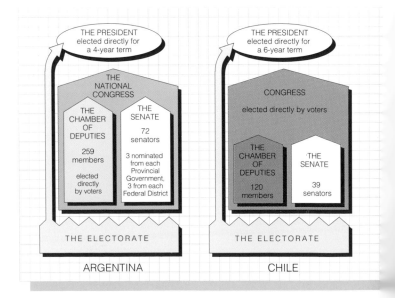

▲ **The death of President Allende of Chile in 1973 is remembered every year. This commemorative procession took place in 1990.**

only 74 days, and the junta soon followed. The country returned to civilian rule first with President Raúl Alfonsín and then with President Carlos Menem. Argentina now has a constitution and democratic elections, and the influence of the army, while still great, is gradually ebbing.

Chile's most famous president was the socialist Salvador Allende, elected in 1970 in the country's first democratically elected government. His reforms nationalized banking, insurance, communications and industry, but this led to hostility from Chile's business community and the USA. In 1973, his government was overthrown in a CIA-backed military coup. Allende, according to

varying reports, either committed suicide or was murdered. General Augusto Pinochet took over and banned all political activity in a brutally repressive regime. This came as a great shock to Chile, which is traditionally a peaceful country. Thousands of Allende's

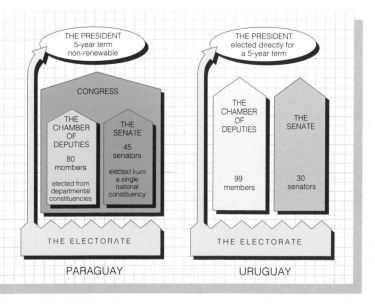

◀ *Alfredo Stroessner was President of Paraguay from 1954–1989 in one of the most corrupt and longest lasting dictatorships in South America.*

supporters were arrested, tortured and executed. All political parties and trade unions were banned. Free elections finally took place again in 1989, although General Pinochet remained as army commander until 1998. Since then, there has been a feeling of liberation throughout the country.

Uruguay started the 20th century with what was a pioneering welfare state compared to the rest of South America.

However, by the mid-1960s, economic problems had caused severe political unrest. This eventually led to a military take-over in 1973. Until 1985, torture became routine and the regime was accused of appalling human rights abuses, with more than 60,000 people detained. Julio María Sanguinetti was elected in 1984, with the military suppressing the other political parties. But, since that time, there has been a gradual loosening of military power.

Paraguay has perhaps suffered the worst regime in all of South America under General Alfredo Stroessner, who ruled the country for 35 years from 1954. This brutal and despotic government had a complete disregard for human rights and permitted no real political opposition. When Stroessner was finally overthrown in 1989, there was a movement to destroy the thousands of monuments built in his honour. In 1992, a constitution was established, although it is still uncertain whether democracy will last.

FOOD AND FARMING

South America, in general, and Argentina, in particular, produce vast quantities of food and products from livestock. Argentina's economy relies heavily on agriculture although, generally, it is a very urban and Europeanized society. It is one of the world's biggest meat and wool producers from the livestock on its huge estancias, that run beef cattle in the north of the country and sheep in the south. Less well known is the fact that Argentina is also the ninth largest producer of cotton in the world and grows vast quantities of oil seeds – such as soya beans, sunflower, cottonseed, groundnuts and grapeseed. Argentina, in fact, produces a total of 19 million tonnes of oil from these crops every year, making it the fifth largest producer in the world. The Argentinian farming industry also exports huge quantities of wheat, wine, maize, sugar, fruit and vegetables, as well as growing these for the home market.

Chile is less dependent on agriculture than Argentina, traditionally growing such crops as cereals, seeds, vegetables and fruit. However, its long Pacific coastline has made fishing an important industry with an annual catch as large as the entire catch of the USA and UK put together, and

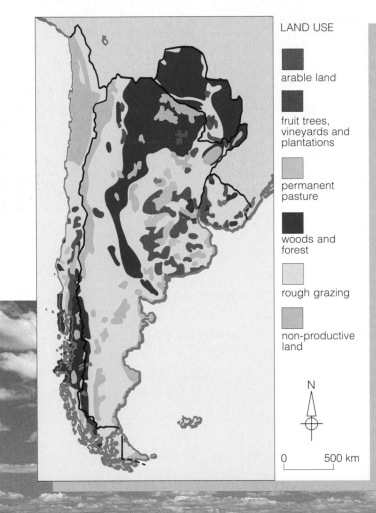

LAND USE

- arable land
- fruit trees, vineyards and plantations
- permanent pasture
- woods and forest
- rough grazing
- non-productive land

N

0   500 km

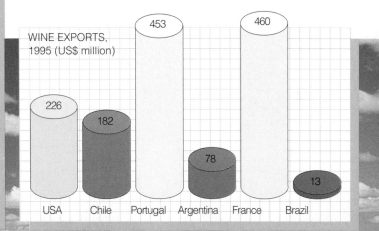

WINE EXPORTS, 1995 (US$ million)

USA	Chile	Portugal	Argentina	France	Brazil
226	182	453	78	460	13

▼ *Talcahuano has the best harbour in Chile and is an important fishing port as well as being the main naval centre in the country.*

KEY FACTS

● Argentina is the 5th largest wool producer and the 10th largest meat producer in the world.
● Chile has a coastline of 5,338 kilometres and exclusive fishing rights over 1,600,000 square kilometres.
● Uruguay's meat processing was pioneered on the coast at Fray Bentos, known worldwide for corned beef.
● Prepared meats are a vital part of the South American economy. Argentina exports US$ 381 million-worth of prepared meats, only just behind the world leader, the USA with US$ 389 million.

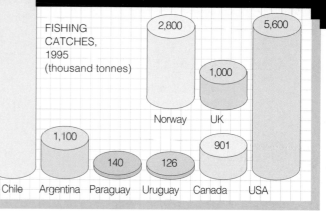

FISHING CATCHES, 1995 (thousand tonnes)

Chile	Argentina	Paraguay	Uruguay	Canada	USA
7,600	1,100	140	126	901	5,600

Norway 2,800   UK 1,000

◄ *Sheep farming is the main industry of Patagonian Argentina and its huge estancias cover thousands of square kilometres.*

including 220 species of edible fish. Chile also has a large wine-making industry. The first vineyard was established by the Spanish in 1551, to supply wine for the religious celebration of the Mass. Because of its natural frontiers of ocean, mountains and desert, Chile has been one of the few countries in the world not to have been affected by the PHYLLOXERA epidemic, which has wiped out vineyards in other countries.

Farming accounts for 25% of the GROSS DOMESTIC PRODUCT of Paraguay and employs 45% of its workforce. Much of this is subsistence farming, with families working small areas of land to feed themselves, and selling the little that is left over at local markets. It does export beef, maize, sugar, timber and cotton but, due to its land-locked position in the middle of the continent, transport costs are high, making its products very expensive.

Uruguay's main industry is farming and, in particular, pastoral farming with cattle and sheep estancias occupying more than three-quarters of the land. Only 10% of the land is devoted to growing crops, although much more could be put under cultivation. Nevertheless, cereals, including rice, make an important contribution to the economy. A wide range of fruit and vegetables is also grown.

One of South America's unique crops is yerba maté, also known as Paraguayan tea. It is grown and drunk throughout the region, but is particularly popular in Argentina. Maté is made from the leaves of a holly-like plant and Argentinians drink about four times as much of it as they do coffee.

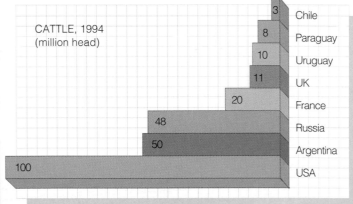

CATTLE, 1994 (million head)

Country	Million head
Chile	3
Paraguay	8
Uruguay	10
UK	11
France	20
Russia	48
Argentina	50
USA	100

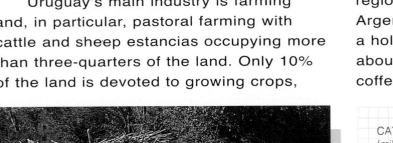

▲ *In the low Chaco of Paraguay, sugarcane is transported by ox-drawn cart, or carreta, to a local market.*

▶ *In the old sector of Montevideo, a greengrocer sets out an appetising array of fruit and vegetables.*

TRADE AND INDUSTRY

Agricultural products, such as foods, oils, leather, wool and cotton play a large part in all South American economies, although this is least true in Chile, where mining and fishing are so important. In Argentina, there is a huge industry based on meat processing, while around 80% of the country's cereal crops are exported. Other industries have advanced rapidly as the country's oil reserves have been exploited. These include the manufacture of paper, steel, cars, textiles and chemicals.

Chile's economy is based principally on the mining of copper, iron ore, gold and silver. Timber and paper are exported in sizeable quantities. For this reason, cultivated forest is taking up increasing areas of the country, although native forest has been declining proportionately. Although agriculture is an important industry in Chile, it does not produce enough food for the country. Great quantities of foodstuffs are, therefore, imported. Manufacturing industries include food processing, metalworking and textiles.

In Paraguay, wood products, cotton and

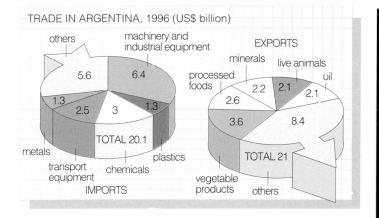

TRADE IN ARGENTINA, 1996 (US$ billion)

IMPORTS: others 5.6, machinery and industrial equipment 6.4, metals 1.3, transport equipment 2.5, chemicals 3, plastics 1.3, TOTAL 20.1

EXPORTS: minerals 2.2, live animals 2.1, oil 2.1, processed foods 2.6, 3.6, 8.4, vegetable products, others, TOTAL 21

KEY FACTS

● In the last decade, privatization of nationalized industries has been widespread throughout the region. Argentina, in particular, has sold off much of the state sector, including the state telephone and oil companies.

● Uruguay is still one of the most state-dominated countries in the region and renowned for its slow and difficult bureaucracy.

● Argentina's industrial output is substantial. It stands at around US$ 85 billion a year.

◀ The beef industry is vital to Argentina's economy. This vast cattle market, on the outskirts of Buenos Aires, stretches as far as the eye can see.

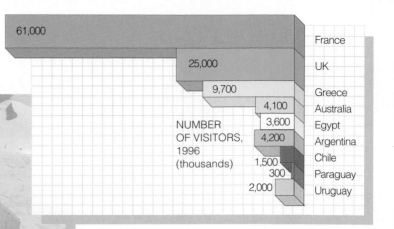

NUMBER OF VISITORS, 1996 (thousands)	
61,000	France
25,000	UK
9,700	Greece
4,100	Australia
3,600	Egypt
4,200	Argentina
1,500	Chile
300	Paraguay
2,000	Uruguay

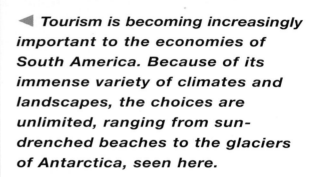

◄ *Tourism is becoming increasingly important to the economies of South America. Because of its immense variety of climates and landscapes, the choices are unlimited, ranging from sun-drenched beaches to the glaciers of Antarctica, seen here.*

cigarettes form the principal industries besides agriculture, while the hydro-electric plants it has built produce a surplus of energy for export to its neighbours. However, Paraguay has suffered because of its land-locked geographical position. This makes its exports very expensive to transport and, therefore, uncompetitive in the world market. Paraguayan workers, in both farming and industry, are very poorly paid and much of the economy is propped up by CONTRABAND, including the trade of illegal drugs.

The Uruguayan economy is essentially based on agriculture, with beef its chief export. Industries include oil refining and the manufacture of cement and textiles, all based around Montevideo. Tourism is particularly important to Uruguay, with many visitors from other Latin American countries. Tourism, in fact, is growing throughout South America and already accounts for around 20% of Argentina's income with many visitors coming from the USA and

▲ *Beautiful silver objects have been produced in Chile and Argentina from very early times. These silver pieces were made in the 20th century.*

Europe, as well as other Latin American countries.

FOREIGN DEBT

In spite of Argentina's high industrial output, it still has one of the highest international

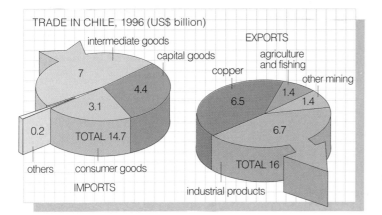

COPPER EXPORTS (ores and concentrates), 1996 (thousand tonnes)

Chile 1,019.8

European Union 876.7

Asia 150.8

World total 3,138.1

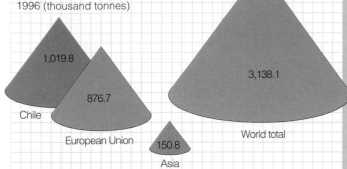

TRADE IN CHILE, 1996 (US$ billion)

IMPORTS

intermediate goods 7

capital goods 4.4

3.1

0.2 others

consumer goods

TOTAL 14.7

EXPORTS

copper 6.5

agriculture and fishing 1.4

other mining 1.4

6.7

industrial products

TOTAL 16

foreign debt, any significant economic development is hampered.

MERCOSUR

In 1995, Mercosur was established, creating a 'Common Market' within the South American nations of Brazil, Argentina, Uruguay and Paraguay. It is based on establishing a free-trade zone to encourage commerce and industry and reduce prices overall. However, there is no free movement of labour allowed among the countries, so many young people in Uruguay and Paraguay have become illegal workers in the neighbouring countries. This deprives their own countries of many of their best workers. In 1996, Chile became an associate member of Mercosur.

debts in the world. The problems of debt and inflation have dogged all of the South American economies for decades. Inflation is still very high in Uruguay, Paraguay and Chile, although Argentina has brought it slightly more under control in recent years. However, with such a high proportion of the countries' incomes spent on servicing

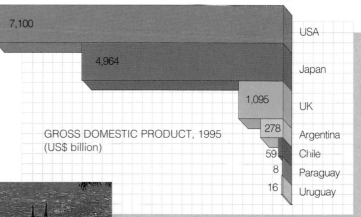

GROSS DOMESTIC PRODUCT, 1995 (US$ billion)

USA	7,100
Japan	4,964
UK	1,095
Argentina	278
Chile	59
Paraguay	8
Uruguay	16

◀ *Valparaiso was founded in 1542 and grew to become the principal port in Chile. After the opening of the Panama Canal in 1914, its position declined. It is still an important fishing and naval port, although its historical buildings have virtually disappeared, as this area has suffered repeated earthquakes.*

The Andes, running down the entire length of South America, more or less divide the land into two parts. Access overland from east to west is limited and at times hazardous. Many of the passes through the mountains between Argentina and Chile become blocked in the winter because of snow. In the summer, however, buses travel through the high passes between these countries and also across the borders of Argentina with Brazil, Bolivia, Uruguay and Paraguay, and from Chile to Bolivia and Peru. In the south of the continent, particularly in Chile, boats are an important means of communication.

Argentina has the best transport system in the region. This includes an extensive domestic air service and a railway network that is the seventh largest in the world. The railway was originally built by the British and has many stations that resemble those of English country towns. There is a similarly extensive road network, covering 216,000 kilometres, nearly all of it hard surfaced. Argentina has one of the highest per capita (per head) car-ownership rates in South America. It also has one of the worst driving records. After 2,000 traffic deaths during only two months in 1995, the problem became known as La Guerra del Transito – 'the traffic war'.

Chile's mountainous terrain, with the Atacama Desert in the north and the fjords and off-shore islands of the south, has made it difficult to develop a good internal

KEY FACTS

● Argentina has 34,200 kilometres of railway network – more than twice that of the UK.
● Traffic accidents are the main cause of death for Argentinians between the ages of 5 and 35.
● Paraguay's capital, Asunción, has an extensive tram network as well as buses.

◀ *Paraguay's tiny rail network uses antiquated wood-burning steam locomotives.*

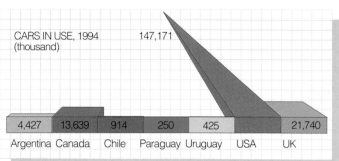

CARS IN USE, 1994 (thousand)					147,171		
4,427	13,639	914	250	425			21,740
Argentina	Canada	Chile	Paraguay	Uruguay	USA		UK

there are freight trains. The roads in the interior of the country are rough and unpaved, and only a few cars travel on them. The most common way of crossing to Argentina is by ferry or hydrofoil from Montevideo and there are also roads across the borders with Brazil and Argentina.

Paraguay has only three border crossings to Argentina, two to Brazil and one to Bolivia. Only 10% of Paraguay's roads are paved, however, and car ownership is low. In the countryside, the horse and ox-carts are still an important form of transport.

▲ **With its high car ownership, the rush hour in Buenos Aires is as busy as that of any capital city, as can be seen in Avenida del Libertador, in the centre of town.**

▼ **In Encarnación, Paraguay's third largest city, the horse and cart is still a common form of transport.**

transport system. Coastal boat services were the main form of transport from one town to the next within Chile until the early 20th century. This is still true in the south. However, there is now an established road network, not all of which is paved, and most Chileans travel by bus or car. Santiago has a good underground railway system and good air links with the rest of the country.

Uruguay has limited domestic air services and no passenger trains, although

THE ENVIRONMENT

▲ *The Lauca National Park in the north of Chile stretches to the frontier with Bolivia and features numerous snowy volcanoes, ten of which are over 6,000 metres high.*

South America, with its vast empty spaces, small population, low industrial output and low car ownership, has little atmospheric pollution when compared to the USA or Europe. However, there are few environmental controls either, and most Latin American governments show little interest in introducing any. One of the main problems is deforestation. In spite of its tiny size, Paraguay is tenth in the world league of deforesters. A great deal of the country is forested but much of the native forest is being replaced by cultivated forest for the timber trade. During the period 1980–1993, more than 36% of Paraguay's natural forest was destroyed. There are a few national parks and nature reserves in the country, but many animals are in danger of extinction. Among them are the giant anteater, the giant armadillo, the jaguar and the pampas deer.

Argentina now has an extensive system of national parks, where a large number of endangered species are protected. These include the Andean condor, the Argentine boa constrictor and a great variety of whales around its shores. However, there have also been some major environmental problems in Argentina. These include industrial pollution near Buenos Aires, dumping of nuclear waste, deforestation and over-grazing in Patagonia.

Chile also has an extensive system of national parks and reserves where native species are protected. The vicuña, a species of llama, was hunted almost to extinction. By 1970, there were only 400 left in the country but, since becoming a

KEY FACTS

● In the mid-1970s, the Chacoan peccary was rediscovered in Paraguay, after being thought extinct for over 50 years.

● Paraguay has 365 species of birds including 21 parrots.

● The llama, alpaca, guanaco and vicuña are all camelids – South American camels.

● Volcanoes are still active in Chile. In 1994, El Laima erupted for the first time in 37 years and spewed ash, lava and smoke all over the Andean lake district. Although three-quarters of a million people live there, no one was killed.

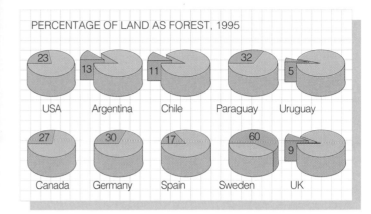

PERCENTAGE OF LAND AS FOREST, 1995

USA	Argentina	Chile	Paraguay	Uruguay
23	13	11	32	5

Canada	Germany	Spain	Sweden	UK
27	30	17	60	9

protected species, numbers have now grown to 12,000. Although no native birds migrate north to the USA, many fly south from North America to spend the summer in the southern hemisphere. There are none of the tropical birds of South America in Chile as it has the wrong terrain for them. Instead, it has the Chilean pigeon and mocking bird in the central area, while in Patagonia, there are steamer ducks, the Humboldt penguin, the Magellanic penguin, the Inca tern and the storm petrel.

▲ The jaguar was once common in the savannas of Chile, but because of hunting it is now an endangered species.

► While part of Argentinian Tierra del Fuego is a national park, there is substantial logging in other parts. This has led to the destruction of whole forests.

THE FUTURE

In recent years, there has been political progress throughout South America. Democracy has returned, at least in some form, to most of the countries and human rights are gradually improving.

The long-term economic problems, however, have not been so easy to solve. In Uruguay, for instance, HYPERINFLATION resulted in the introduction of two new currencies in the space of 20 years. In 1996, Uruguay's inflation was running at over 40%, and Paraguay's around 45%, although these figures are low compared to those from just a few years earlier.

At the root of these problems is a combination of government corruption, mismanagement and the immense foreign debt facing South America. Because these debts are so massive, huge sums of money are needed to service them (to pay off the

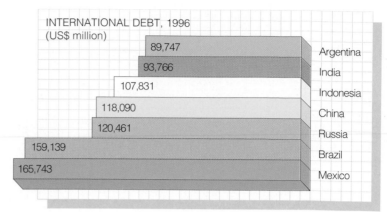

INTERNATIONAL DEBT, 1996
(US$ million)

89,747	Argentina
93,766	India
107,831	Indonesia
118,090	China
120,461	Russia
159,139	Brazil
165,743	Mexico

interest so that the sum originally borrowed does not grow any bigger). The interest payments run at an average of 40% of the entire export earnings of these countries. When added to capital repayments, this rises to 60% of all foreign earnings. In effect, it is impossible to repay the debts and they simply get bigger every year. In the long term, Latin America's only real hope is for

▲ **US President Bill Clinton congratulates Chilean President Eduardo Frei for his opening speech at the second Summit of the Americas, 18 April 1998. One of the main issues for discussion is free trade.**

◄ **A new shopping mall in Montevideo, Uruguay, has been built on the site of a former high security prison where many political prisoners were once detained.**

agreement to be reached among the world's richer nations to cancel out third-world debt.

The economic problems are made worse by the fact that, because of the instability of their countries, South Americans take their money out of their countries to invest it abroad. As the profits from economic success are not ploughed back in, new industry is not generated. Thus the gap between poor and rich continues to grow.

Despite all these problems, South America has many advantages. It is a land that is rich in natural resources, with a vibrant and optimistic people. It is to be hoped that, in the future, Argentina, Chile, Paraguay and Uruguay will be able to develop their very great potential.

KEY FACTS

● The Yacyreta dam in Paraguay – the largest in the world – started production of hydro-electric power in 1994. At peak capacity, it can produce 2,700 megawatts of electricity. This is equivalent to the output of three average-sized nuclear power stations.
● Uruguay has signed trade agreements with China and Russia in an attempt to avoid economic dependence on its giant neighbours, Argentina and Brazil.

FURTHER INFORMATION

● THE ARGENTINE EMBASSY
65 Brook Street, London W1
Provides information on Argentina.

● EMBASSY OF CHILE
12 Devonshire Street, London W1
Provides information on Chile.

● EMBASSY OF PARAGUAY
Braemar Lodge, Cornwall Gardens, London SW7
Provides information on Paraguay.

● URUGUAYAN CONSULATE
140 Brompton Road, London SW3
Provides information on Uruguay.

BOOKS ABOUT THE REGION
Continents: South America, Ewan McLeish,
Wayland 1996 (age 10+)
The People Atlas, Dr Brunetto Chiarelli and
Anna Lisa Bebi, Macdonald Young Books
1997 (age 8+)

GLOSSARY

ALTIPLANO
A Spanish word meaning 'high plain'. It is used
to describe the expanse of high level land in the
Andes region.

CONQUISTADORES
The Spanish conquerors of South America who
arrived in the 16th century.

CONTRABAND
Illegal trade.

COUPS
Violent or illegal changes in government.

DEFORESTATION
The clearance of trees in order to use the land
for a different purpose.

ESTANCIAS
Vast ranches for rearing sheep or cattle.

FIESTA
The Spanish word for party or celebration.

GROSS DOMESTIC PRODUCT
The total value of all the goods and services
produced by a country in a year, apart from
money earned from investments abroad.

HYPERINFLATION
Extreme inflation which occurs when the
currency drops in value so rapidly over a period
of time that prices can rise on a daily basis.

INCAS
Indians, who originally came from the area
around Cuzco in Peru. By the 15th century they
had built a huge empire in South America,
which stretched up to the borders of Columbia
and Ecuador and covered much of Chile and
Bolivia.

INDIGENOUS POPULATION
The original inhabitants of a particular region.

JUNTA
A military dictatorship.

LAND-LOCKED
A country or area that has no coastline. Land-
locked countries are highly dependent on their
neighbours to reach coastal ports, which are
important for trade and industry.

PAMPAS
Flat grassy plains.

PHYLLOXERA
An insect pest that lives on the roots of the vine
and kills it. In the 1870s it destroyed nearly all
the European vineyards. The roots of the native
American vine are immune to this pest.

SAVANNAS
Tropical and sub-tropical vegetation consisting
of grasses, shrubs and scattered trees. It is
typically dry for most of the year but bursts into
life when the first rains arrive.